This book was compiled as an offering for the Vyasa Puja celebration of my spiritual master, 2016.

AF286738

For comments or inquiries, any reader is hereby warmly invited to correspond with the author:

tilakapublishing@gmail.com

Herstellung und Verlag:
BoD - Books on Demand, Norderstedt
ISBN 978-3-8370-8197-8

Writing in Relation to
Krishna consciousness,
volume 4:

The Hermit and his cave,
and
other poems

Invocation

Invocation

"There is nothing within the teachings of Lord Caitanya which is not intelligable by human reasoning, or is against any religious feeling accepted by the civilized society of the world."

(Srila Prabhupada, from the prospectus for The League of devotees, Jhansi, 16th of May 1953.)

Dedication

To all the vaishnavas of the world, who are living examples of Lord caitanya's sankirtan prophecy.

To my spiritual master, who exemplifies the process of devotional service within the reach of my eyes' vision.

To Srila Prabhupada, the true wellwisher of all living entities in the entire universe.

Foreword

Before commencing with this writing endeavor, I want to make a pledge to you, dear reader. You are the receiver of these words. You are my intended target.

However, do not be alarmed, for I honestly seek only your benefit. Whatever blessings I may have gathered through the course of my aspiring devotional career, I now present to you.

Furthermore, my pledge to you is to present an honest account of spiritual life, as I observe and experience it. As I have heard it from authorities and read in the scriptures.

This is guaranteed to be a limited presentation, due to my conditioned nature, but in the spiritual sense of the matter, it is actually of little consequence. If the spiritual master is pleased with the disciple, Krishna is pleased, thereby eliminating the need for any endeavor towards perfection in ones activities by one's own strength. This is the great blessing of the sadhus, of the persons dear to our Lord. They have won His heart through selflessness, a quality unheard of, at least to me, in my current existence in this so called modern day and age, that so much professed peak of civilization and culture, in which we now inhabit.

Please forgive my somewhat denigrating tone, dear reader, but as I am now bound by my twice spoken pledge to you, it is my duty to speak the truth as I have seen it, and I am therefore compelled to pour out from those hidden vaults of the heart. Please again excuse me, for my faith in this make believe society has been shaken, by my devotional experience, even though it may be tiny and insignificant. Even the most famished sense of sanity must have observed this? The reality that this world is burning, in the fire of our own desires!

True insanity is indeed the need to hide this most basic of tendencies, namely the courage to question the authoritative foundations of the truths that are imposed upon us, the wayward peoples, truths taken for granted only due to a misplaced faith in material scholars and scientists. How crazy is it to harbor a compelling need to accept and obey the broadcasted reality of the asura leaders of the earth, on grounds of an illusory state of comfort alone? This o'so cherished state of wellbeing, imagined by the common man to be the very pinnacle of self- preservation in the name of enjoyment, this act of complete dullness, so prevalent amongst our human peers, of seeking shelter of ignorance in the hope of facilitating pleasures without the bitter aftertaste of life's realities, birth and death, spoiling our pathetic endeavors. That is just plain crazy.

I refuse to be a sheep in the flock tended by vicious wolves. Time wasted in this way results only in the curse of prolonged identification with the need for sensual pleasures, the curse of attachment to the sense of submission under the iron heel of the contaminated mind.

Dear reader, forgive me, but I have chosen this rebellion, these words, because I too am cursed. However, having tasted the bitterness of material reality, through the medium of guru's enlightenment, I now seek shelter in the service of krishna's devotees, of which my immediate source of such service is my spiritual master.

> "This writing is something very good. I am happy about that and I think you should develop this more and more and write an honest account of spiritual life."

> (Excerpt from letter received by email, 27th of January, 2012.)

This has become my mission, which in due course has developed into a sort of obsession. To contribute something, against the current of the tide of time, seeking to race us towards life's end, without cessation.

Realizing the need to rectify my existence, I write now for purification. If by chance, or by krishna's grace, a reader may find some lesson on (or towards) the road of devotional service, I consider this endeavor a great success.

Hare krishna.

Selected Poems

A day like any other, or.. ? (25.9.2014)

Got to bed
late.
The affairs of
family life
kept me busy.
Then there was
the quite
extensive
pile of dish wash
in the temple kitchen.
Entering my apartment,
putting Their Lordships
to rest,
then singing Gaura Arati
softly
as a lullaby.

No time for reading
Bhagavatam.
Just tired.

Alarm at six,

rise from
slumber at seven.
Bathroom routine,
Gayatri,
obeisances to the
spiritual master.

No time for puja.
Will have to be rescheduled
for this evening.

> "In my mind
> I apologize to
> Their Lordships,
> Sri Sri Pancha Tattva,
> and pray they will
> understand.
>
> They're in
> my heart..."

Making breakfast
and lunch
in one,
wearing jacket
and backpack,
as I cut bread
and mix
yogurt with

cashews, honey
and grated coconut.

chanting one round
going to metro,
realizing at the
end of the round
that one is supposed
to listen to the
names of the mantra,
not curse oneself
in the mind.

Suddenly,
I stop in my tracks...

"This is a test.
This is a test!
It's all arranged,
I can feel it."

Tears well up
in my eyes.

"That means
Krishna is
there,
personally
intervening."

This is an
opportunity
to turn the
tables,
and prove myself
in the face of
obstacles.
To be meek and
mild.
To see krishna's
hands
in my everyday
dealings.
To surrender to
the fact
of the need for
surrender
in my life,
this one life,
for guru and krishna,
and the sankirtan mission
of Lord caitanya.
Today.
Tomorrow.
Forever.

And so,
hope appears
on the horizon

of my
stone like
heart.

I smile
in the midst
of adverse
conditions.

I remember
Arjuna,
and I realize
what has to
be done.

Now go do it!

I exit the metro
and mount the stairs
going to my
bus stop,
facing the chill
of the bright, white,
late autumn sun.

Spiritual hope
is a
truth.

A desperate plea. (2.11.2014)

My dear Gaura Nitai,
is it possible
to completely change
ones life?
Is it too late
for one like me?

Although I have been
around your movement
for almost twenty years,
I have in all honesty
wasted most of my time.

I would like now
to reevaluate my
position and engagements,
with your permission.

In truth,
I have become an
overeating,
lazy, self indulging

slob, and
I am tired of it.

Is it possible
for someone like me
to take repossession
of this yantra,
and manage it nicely
for the service of
guru and Gauranga?

This is surely
a materially tinged
request,
but I am
desperate!

Please help me...

It is not possible
without your help.

Everything is possible
with your mercy.

Time is running out.

All blessings
and good fortune

are in the now,
in activity.

Please help me...

undeserving,
completely
baffled and
helpless,
I hereby submit
this prayer.

A dream of the spiritual master. (18.11.2014)

"A quite sensuous dream ensues after going
to bed late, having taken a sumptuous meal.
Suddenly Gururmaharaja comes in,
the scene of the dream shifts.

"What are you doing?"

He is standing there. I see him clearly.
Brushing him off, in my hazy state, the
dreamy passion continuous.
Again he is there.

"What are your doing? Start running!"

Again I brush him off, to get back into the
dream. A third time he comes.

"Ok, I'm leaving."

The dream is about to peak,
but how can I leave Maharaja aside for a
mere dream?"

I awake. Time is 2 am. I feel a strong urge t o engage my mind so as not to slip back into the dream. Rising from bed, I pick up the Bhagavatam and read, walking back and forth to prevent sleep, for maybe half an hour. Feeling quite refreshed, I take a shower and start my japa. Continuing to chant softly on my beads, I push on until Mangal Artik. Dream fades, but my impression of Gurumaharaja remains clear:

"What are you doing? Start running!"

Why indulge or escape in the mind?
Be serious.
Mind should be controlled
by engagement.

Make the effort.
Be a good disciple.

A moment of truth. (16.5.2015, Saturday)

There is fatigue,
yes,
no doubt.

There is bewilderment
in my mind,
oh yes,
quite right.

There is lack of
devotion,
ha ha,
certainly true.

Can progress
still be made?

Is the mercy
still available?
Maybe most
importantly,
should I take

this chance,
the chance offered
by Srila Prabhupada
on behalf of
Lord caitanya?

undoubtedly
yes!
Yes, of course.

why?

For there is really
nothing else,
nothing else than
activities in devotional service,
somehow engaging
for helping in the spreading
of the holy names
of krishna:

> "Hare krishna, Hare krishna,
> krishna krishna, Hare Hare,
> Hare Rama, Hare Rama,
> Rama Rama, Hare Hare."

I emerge,
pen in hand.
I find myself

in the association
of the devotees of krishna.

There is a room
in one house,
surrounded by a
small garden.
It is my house.

In this room
there is a gathering
of vaishnavas.
A lecture
is going on.
There is a festival.
The walls still vibrate
from a few hours
of ecstatic kirtan.

I am little
in the back,
having exited
the kitchen,
sitting now,
notebook on my
right knee.
Even now,
my hand drives the pen
forward,

crooked letters,
crow's signs.

Finally,
having purged my mind
through an attempt at
devotional record,
I break off
and focus in on
the words being spoken.

Please excuse me,
dear reader,
for I must end.

I will take
this
chance.

Meditation on mercy (7:15 am, 29.9.14)

I snap out
of a dream.

Ate some sweets
before taking
rest
last night,
late.
Result was some
bizarre
illicid adventure.

I snap out
of a dream.

Laying on the
bed,
I am confused.
Overwhelmed
in the moment,
drenched
in the lower modes,

conditioned mind
kindled.
I hesitate,
due to weakness
of heart.

My world
freezes
for a fraction
of a
heartbeat.

Then there is
a voice
from inside:

"wake up from
the dream,
to a work
in progress."

I snap out
of
the dream.

On the metro (2.10.14)

Will I ever
become steady?
Maybe more
importantly,
will I ever
befriend
the mind?

This is
without a doubt,
my life's
greatest challenged,
for I am
heavily
conditioned
by sinful choice
and deed.

Problem
identified,
solution
must now be

addressed,
for to focus on
problem only
is an act of
selfish indulgence.
It creates an
environment
for cultivating
excuses.
It belittles
the position of
Krishna as the
ever kind Lord,
arranging all things
for our fatherly
correction,
our ultimate
salvation,
progress on the
path of devotional service.

As emotions
boil,
and a broken heart's
guilt
fuels the fire of
regret,
to engage in
acts of surrender

seems impossible.

However,
the word
impossible
breaks up into two
interesting
parts:
    I'm
    possible.

How so?

By the grace of
guru and Gauranga

    "guru krishna
    prasade bhaya
    bhakti lata bhija",

and maintaining
free will's
activities,
alike the work
of a gardener,
always
tending,
cultivating,
mindful of weeds and bugs,

of the separatist spirit,
intellect soaked
in free indulgence
of the mind
and senses.

what is
sadhana?

A foundation
to build
the impenetrable fortress of
rising early
to chant
good rounds.

Embrace
the devotee lifestyle,
so by feeding
spiritual intelligence
with an effort
in goodness,
the willpower
of the soul
dawns to subdue
the mind
with the sweetness
of krishna consciousness.

Rediscovering the path (or Forest trek with a friend, 30.9.14)

"You know
you had
a good fire
the evening before,
when you can
rekindle it
without
matches in the
morning."

Awake,
nature calls.
Fueling the fire
is first priority.

As the flames
soar,
I do my business,
then dive into the
quite cold,
yet very refreshing

lake,
huddling
before the friendly
fire
after.

Now,
dressed in wool,
japa awaits,
then porridge
for breakfast.

After that,
finding my way
home,
through the
winding paths
of the
forrest of illusion,
the material world.

Rediscovering vrindavan, part 3. (21.10.2014, Srila
Prabhupada's disappearance day)

My pace is
somewhat quick.
Time is over 5pm,
so there is not
so much left
of day's light,
but I remain
determined,
by the grace of
guru and Gauranga.

I am on a
mission
of personal nature.

By now,
after repeated visits
to this holy place
vrindavan,
I have a
favorite route

and a few
places
I always visit.

This evening
however,
one of my destinations
is an unfamiliar one,
a place I have yet
to seek out.

Again I traverse
through
quiet back alleys,
through
village like neighborhoods,
where wood is stacked
on rooftops,
for drying,
or for monkey protection,
I cannot tell.
A plain doorway,
like any other dwelling,
reveals an open space
housing a goshala.
Oblivious cows
roam as they please.
More condensed
crowds signals

entrance into
the bazar.

My business
is not with
wallas or
merchants,

    I am seeking
    mercy.

Passing a familiar place,
I do a short
detour, to stand before
a friendly face:
Lord Narashima,
the only of His kind
in vrindavan.

I am kindly greeted
by the Lord,
being all
broad, furry smile,
seated together
with Prahlad and Laxmidevi.
Presenting myself
before Him,
I shortly take in
His mustachio,

tongue poking darshan.

I continue on
my mission.

Further on,
into the thick of the
congestion,
hidden within
a small doorway,
between a jewler and
a chai stand,
I find my first
destination:

> The worshipable
> deities of
> Murari Gupta,
> Sri Sri Gaura Nitai.

It is my
first time
here.

Lord Nityananda holds
His palm up,
showering blessings,
while Lord Gauranga
holds His right hand

in a mudra, left hand
to his side.

I stay for some time
chanting japa,
facing the Brothers,
in the end rewarded
with permission
to take a photo.

My mission
continues.

I leave for Mayapura Dhama
in two days,
so I must make
the effort
to visit Rupa Goswami,
or my stay in
Braja
is not complete.
This was the
instruction
given to me
by Smita Krishna Swami.

Arriving at last,
the dark of the
vrindavan evening

descends.

crowd is huge!
Parikrama is all
pushing and shoves,
however
I see this as a
test of eagerness
only.
Srila Prabhupada
has come out of
his rooms
to give darshan
and all the devotees
literally
shower him
with flowers.

In front of Rupa Goswami
is a crowd of western devotees,
probably from South America,
led by bearded
sannyasis.
From what I understand
they sing songs
glorifying Srila Prabhupada,
one devotee holding
his garlanded picture,
held high in

reverence.

I had hoped
for a more
private darshan,
but it is not
to be.
Still,
I am content.

Relishing the bhajans,
I sit quietly in
a corner,
writing this
poem.

Offering obeisances,
I take my leave,
returning home
in the dark,

    my mission complete.

The hermit and his cave. (22.12.2014)

I am a hermit,
living in the cave
of my own
mind.

You become quite
articulate,
from listening
all day long
to that voice,
always speaking,
speculating,
contemplating.

However,
it is a lonely
reality.

Why?
Because Krishna
is not
manifest

there.

why would He
go there?
There is no room
for Him.
I take up too much
space
in my narrow mindedness.

I need to
get out more.

Harinama is
nice.
The cave lights up,
and there are
people, devotees.

From the platform
of engagement
for the spreading of
the holy names of
krishna,
any dwelling can
be utilized.

kings can embrace
the peoples

of this world.

Sadhus can
change the hearts
of the wayward.

A hermit
can leave his
cave
and venture into
the villages of
simple folk,
and maybe,
by interacting
with a few souls,
by sharing something,
a longing for Krishna,
his life may be granted
value,
purpose.

And although
the world outside
the cave
is a strange one,
in which a hermit
may feel misplaced,
much because of his
awkward appearance,

speaking in riddles, or
broken sentences,
having spent all those years
in that remote cave,
his heart always dwelling
on the secluded comfort
of the rocky floor
and the moldy walls,
he may dare
to go beyond,
and leave the cave behind
altogether.

This prospect,
to die and part,
far, far away
from the solace
of the cave,
certainly seems
truly unnatural
for a hermit,

> but if it pleases
> krishna and
> the spiritual master,
> this hermit
> hereby pledges his life
> to that service.

untitled, (28.9.14)

I am a demon.
Full fledged,
real life
demon.

You may not
see it,
but you are looking
with the wrong kind of
eye.

can you not
see my
subtle horns?

can you not
feel my
flaming
ethereal breath?
My stone hard
scales,
the touch of my

razor like
psychic
claws?

Born in
m'leccha desh,
I am accustomed
to tear at the
flesh of the
emotions
of those around me.

And although
seemingly engaged
in bhakti,
I am a pretender devotee.
I serve only
in a grudging
mood.

What can be done?

Even
Vibhishan
was a great devotee.
He took shelter
of Lord Ramachandra.
Remember now
Prahlad Maharaja

and
King Bali!

Engage
the demon.
Purge him
through the process
of devotional service.

"This morning
I am alone
preparing
the Sunday Feast,
expecting forty,
or so,
guests.

I am late to rise,
so there is only
eleven rounds
before puja.

However,
I am caught
off-guard.
My Pancha Tattva
are cool
to the touch,
so soothing.

This morning
I bathe Them in
silence, not
saying my usual
mantras.

Gaura Nitai
observe me,
as I push on
and do the
mechanics.

Bhoga offering,
and while
The Lords partake
in plums
and assorted nuts,
I am urged from
within
to write this
poem."

voices in the ether, or Board the boat. (undated, 2015)

voices
in the
ether.

Some call
from a distance,
seemingly enticing
devotion.

Others whisper
of opportunities
for pleasure.

Still others
indicate
a need for
attention,
or else...

Real voices.
Real words.
Real feelings.

Real tests.

I must
go on
undisturbed.

I must
see beyond
the ghostly faces,
beyond
lucid dreams
and their
suggestive
attempts.

Above all,
I must go on,
serving loyally
in this ISKCON,
this jnana-palvena,
this boat of transcendental knowledge.

These voices,
the mind,
must be engaged.
If not by
love of Krishna,
then by
transcendental knowledge.

Board the boat.
Serve on the deck,
come storm, or
calm seas.

> When Fritjof Nansen[1] sailed for the North Pole
> in 1893, his vessel, Fram, was constructed in
> such a fashion that the screwing of the polar
> ice could not break it down. Rather, instead of
> being crushed, the boat would be pressed up,
> much like a piece of soap is squeezed between
> wet hands.

This boat
will not
capsize.

Board it,
serve it,
and live your life
in peace.

---

1   (1861-1930) Norwegian explorer, statesman and scientist.

work about to commence. In the car. (5.8.2015)

Sigh,
there are many a
discrepancy
in my life
and character.
There is ample
reason
to despair.

However,
I have my
service.
This is my
saving grace.

I have a
connection with
Krishna
through the medium
of my spiritual master.
This is my
solace.

when times
are tough,
when the mind
revolts,
when the season
of reactions
are in their
winter phase,
this is the time
when I
should count
my blessings,
when I should
take shelter
in scriptures,
in service,
in sanga.
This is a time
for japa,
for kirtan
and
recorded lectures.

Honestly,
these are times
when I can
truly
prove myself,

"Sukhinah Ksatriyah",

to be equipoised
in the face of obstacles,
and just do my
duty,
just serve
regardless
of outcome,
and rest assured
that I am
situated
in my rightful
position

    as a servant
    in the line of
    disciplic succession.

As a matter
of fact,
this is a great
boon,
like the benedictions
of old,
of bygone ages.

It is a weapon,
to cut down

the illusions of
doubt and
false prestige.

Draw now
your sword
and face
the beast
in your mind.

Once, when Srila Prabhupada was very ill,
there was a function to be held. An opening
of a temple. Actually the temple was not
finished. It was an opening, just for the sake
of opening. A governor was to attend the
ceremony. (I guess this was in India.) His
servant recollects that Srila Prabhupada was
to sick to even speak, and although the
devotees pleaded with him to remain in bed
Srila Prabhupada said only: "I want to fight
like Arjuna, and die on the battlefield." Srila
Prabhupada walked out of his room, shaking
like a leaf, and spoke for ten minutes, just
for the sake of this governor. And everyone
present testified that the voice coming out of
Srila Prabhupada's mouth was unearthly. It
had nothing to do with his regular voice.

Fight!

And if needed,

"svarga dvaram apavritam,"

die a
glorious death
on the
battlefield
of preaching.

Raw from the notebook

Oslo I (22.12.2014)

My spiritual master
told me in vrindavan
to get off the
jnana mishra platform.

Alas,
if he only knew
what these words
would imply.

I would have to
change my whole
life around.
change everything!

It is a
transcendental trick
to force me into
submission.
To concur
with guru's instruction,
the crown jewel

of personal guidance,
I will have to
become a devotee
and surrender.

Alas,
I am now
trapped in a
prison of service,
and Lord Caitanya
has slammed the door
shut.

Alas,
what kind mercy.

Oslo 2 (27.1.2015, exactly 4 pm.)

Have you ever
had the
feeling
that there is
something
going on
behind the scene
of life?

I have it
all the time.

Like I'm in a
script,
even now
at this point in time,
unfolding,
to serve as a record
of the ongoing
evolution
of puranic
time.

waves of
black ink
to flood the
parchment filled
volume
that is this world.

That is
this poem.

warsawa (3.1.2015.)

"observing a festival in an unfamiliar
environment gives the blessing of observation
of own conditions, as like from a distance."

Suddenly,
I wake up
to a
heart.

Taken
aback,
I don't know
what to do.

I am so
used to
living in
the mind.

The warmth
of a heart's
desire

is a surprise.

I want to
immediately engage,
but I
can't.

I want to
immediately confess,
but there is
no one in
the moment.

All I can do
is to register
and record,
hoping that
future revelations
find me stronger,
more aware,
more surrendered.

And so
the broken heart
leaves the
experience behind,
to continue.
But,
although the heart

is broken,
the continuation
heralds will
and purpose.

what remains
is a
broken hope
of reinstatement,

purpose fulfilled,
will dovetailed.

Oslo 3 (or The friend that was lost, 27.6.2015)

I know what
it is like to be
lost at sea.

When the ocean
of material existence
expands
from the size of a
calf's hoof print,
into a vast
and unfathomable
watery body,
all hope of crossing
is lost
in the surging waves
of threefold miseries.

There might be
the occasional buoy,
random log
floating around,
or some lonely
atoll,

like economic prosperity
sensual pleasures,
or liberation,
but in a tossing
gigantuan body of
raging water,
their solace are rendered
null and void.

I realize
that only
the outstretched hand
of guru and Gauranga,
venturing the seas
of this world,
can save us.

Their ship
with it's thousands
of masts
and qualified crew,
always watchful
on jewel bedecked decks,
is in reality
this society for
Krishna consciousness,
and the helmsman,
Srila Prabhupada,
is supremely competent

to navigate the
rocking seas
of this world,
to bring any
wayward jiva
to the safe haven
of devotional service.

From there
this gurgling ocean
will again shrink,
to be filled into
no more
than the hoof print
of a calf,
so that we can
step over
and beyond,
into real life,
with Krishna,

our dear most friend.

Afterword

Although the opening words that greeted you, dear reader, were somewhat fiery, through the process of attempted devotional expression, my passion has found engagement and purification. Thank you for taking the time to read this through.

My initial idea for this publication was to yield defeat and put all my cards on the table. No more bluffing. And as I explored the ink filled notebooks of this years record, I became inspired.

This is not my achievement, however it truly is the result of taking the time to actually listen when attending lectures, and endeavoring to do at least some regular service, for the sake of pushing forward the sankirtan mission of Lord caitanya, however mental, or pressed for time one may find oneself.

Whatever it be, I learned this from my spiritual master, to say yes to devotees, and just jump into it. Take a chance on mercy. The result is up to Krishna, but in the end it is always enlightening and amazing. Something to remember. Something that was not a waste, but rather an investment in spiritual life, in the devotional service of Krishna.

In ending, please do not think that I have forgotten my pledge, twice spoken between the beginning pages above. Again therefore, invoking the auspicious third mention of my promise, to award you with the collected blessings I have received, I hereby present them to you.

Will it have any effect? I cannot tell, because the realm of divinity is not available to be evaluated by my conditioned perception. My existence is a life lived as a tiny spec only, in the grand scheme of truth's reality.

Still, I desire to present you with a gift, one that would serve to uplift you in some, or any, way toward the lotus like solace of engagement in devotional service. Poor, spiritually famished, yet happily situated as a beggar for mercy, I offer you this small gift, the gift of honest expression.

Hare Krishna.